THE GOLD RUSH
The Uses and Importance of Gold

Chemistry Book for Kids 9-12
Children's Chemistry Books

Speedy Publishing LLC

40 E. Main St. #1156

Newark, DE 19711

www.speedypublishing.com

Copyright 2017

All Rights reserved. No part of this book may be reproduced or used in any way or form or by any means whether electronic or mechanical, this means that you cannot record or photocopy any material ideas or tips that are provided in this book

In this book, we're going to talk about the uses and importance of the element of gold. So, let's get right to it!

79

Au

2
8
18
32
18
1

Gold

196.966569

THE FACTS ABOUT GOLD

The element of gold is abbreviated as Au, which comes from the Latin word for gold, "aurum," meaning glowing dawn. Its atomic number is 79, which means it has 79 protons. Its phase is solid when it's at room temperature and it has a melting point of 1,947 degrees Fahrenheit and a boiling point of 5,173 degrees Fahrenheit.

It's classified as a transition metal, which simply means it is both ductile and malleable. Gold only has one stable isotope that occurs naturally. That isotope is gold-197. No one knows who discovered gold since it's always been on Earth and people have used it since ancient times.

CHARACTERISTICS OF GOLD

In its natural state, gold is a yellow metal that's shiny. At about 19.3 grams per cubic centimeter, gold is dense, which also makes it heavy. At the same time, it's very soft.

It's the most malleable of all the Earth's metals, which simply means it's flexible enough in its pure form to be pounded out very, very thinly. It's also the most ductile of all Earth's metals, which simply means that it can be made into the thinnest wires that will conduct both heat and electricity.

Gold also reflects heat and light very well. Astronaut's helmets have an incredibly thin layer of gold, about 0.000002 inches, on their visors. The gold is so thin that it's transparent, but even at that level of thinness it helps to decrease glare as well as heat from the sun.

HOW IS GOLD USED?

Almost all gold, over 78% of the gold that is mined yearly, is used to create jewelry. Manufacturing, medical, and dental industries use about 12% yearly as well. The other 10% is used for monetary transactions. In addition to being beautiful and valuable, gold has some other scientific properties that make it an essential element in many types of manufacturing.

For example, in the industry of electronics, it's used as a contact metal because it's an excellent conductor of both heat and electricity. Even though the elements of copper and silver conduct heat and electricity better than gold does, connections made with gold last longer, because they don't tarnish like copper and silver do. Gold doesn't necessarily last longer. It just retains its conductivity longer since it doesn't tarnish or corrode when it's exposed to either air or water.

WHERE IS GOLD FOUND ON EARTH?

Gold is rare on Earth and that's one of the reasons it's considered to be valuable. Scientists believe that gold is formed naturally from a mixture of liquids and gases that come from deep inside the Earth. It reaches the Earth's surface through cracks and faults in the Earth's crust. It's an element in the veins of rocks and is frequently found mixed with silver in a natural alloy that is called electrum.

Gold deposits can be found in the same area or inside the same formation of rock. Miners work hard to find these types of gold deposits. There are three types of gold deposits. The first type is called a primary deposit. The second type is called a secondary deposit and the third type is called a Carlin-type of deposit, named after the first miner who discovered it.

Gold Mining

Where there is a concentration of gold on the interior of a rock, it's called a primary deposit. There are two types of primary deposits: lode and intrusion related. Lode deposits are formed when Earth's tectonic plates are forced on top of each other. They start piling up and over millions of years mountain ranges form.

During this process, extremely hot water bubbles up from under the ground and flows into the cracks. This water is rich in minerals as well as elements. When the water gradually cools down, it can't hold the minerals any more and they begin to filter out and deposit themselves in the rock's fissures. In lode deposits, gold is often found with quartz.

Intrusion related deposits are formed by hot magma deep inside the Earth. As the magma starts to cool, it creates igneous rock. Sometimes as the magma pushes its way to the surface, it brings extremely hot water with it. Just as with the lode deposits, when the water cools down, the minerals are filtered out. Even though the magma is intensely hot, the water doesn't boil away because it's under so much pressure.

Secondary deposits of gold occur because of erosion. The gold is carried by water from its primary location to a different location. Water breaks the

rock into pieces and gold deposits in the form of nuggets are carried downstream. These types of deposits are called placer deposits.

The people who came looking for gold during the California Gold Rush were able to find gold this way. They searched for gold by filling up pans and carefully sifting out the gold from other materials. Gold is heavier than the other sediments and remains at the bottom of the pan. Eventually, the primary deposits were found and those were mined for gold as well.

Carlin-type deposits are formed in a similar way as the other types of deposits. These deposits are located in sedimentary rocks. The gold veins in these deposits are so small that they can't be seen with the naked eye.

Sedimentary Rocks

The gold-bearing sedimentary rock has to be pulverized and chemicals must be used to collect the gold. There

is probably a lot of gold that is as yet undiscovered hiding in Carlin-type deposits.

The other place that gold is found is in ocean water. However, currently the process for extracting gold from seawater is too expensive to be practical.

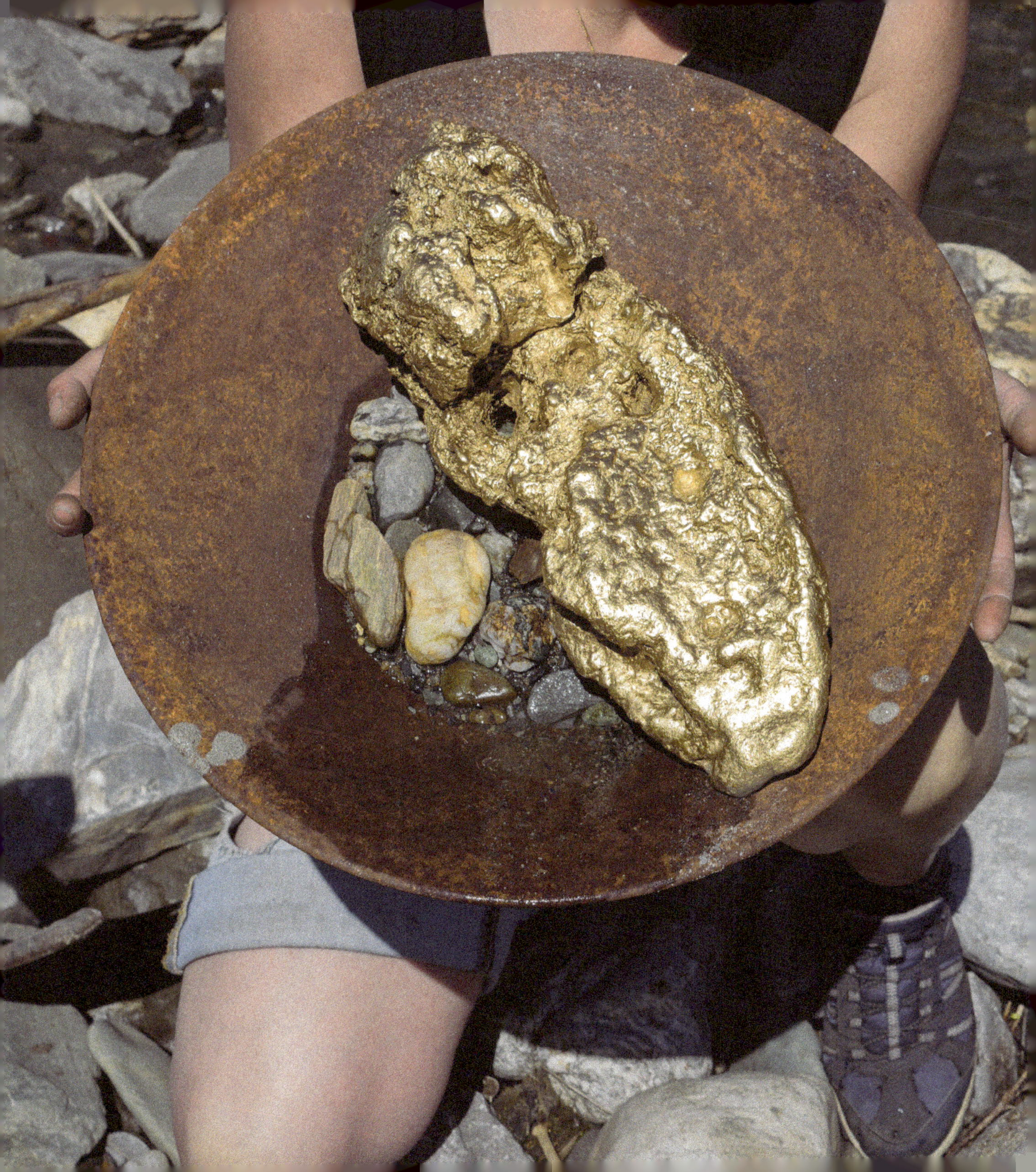

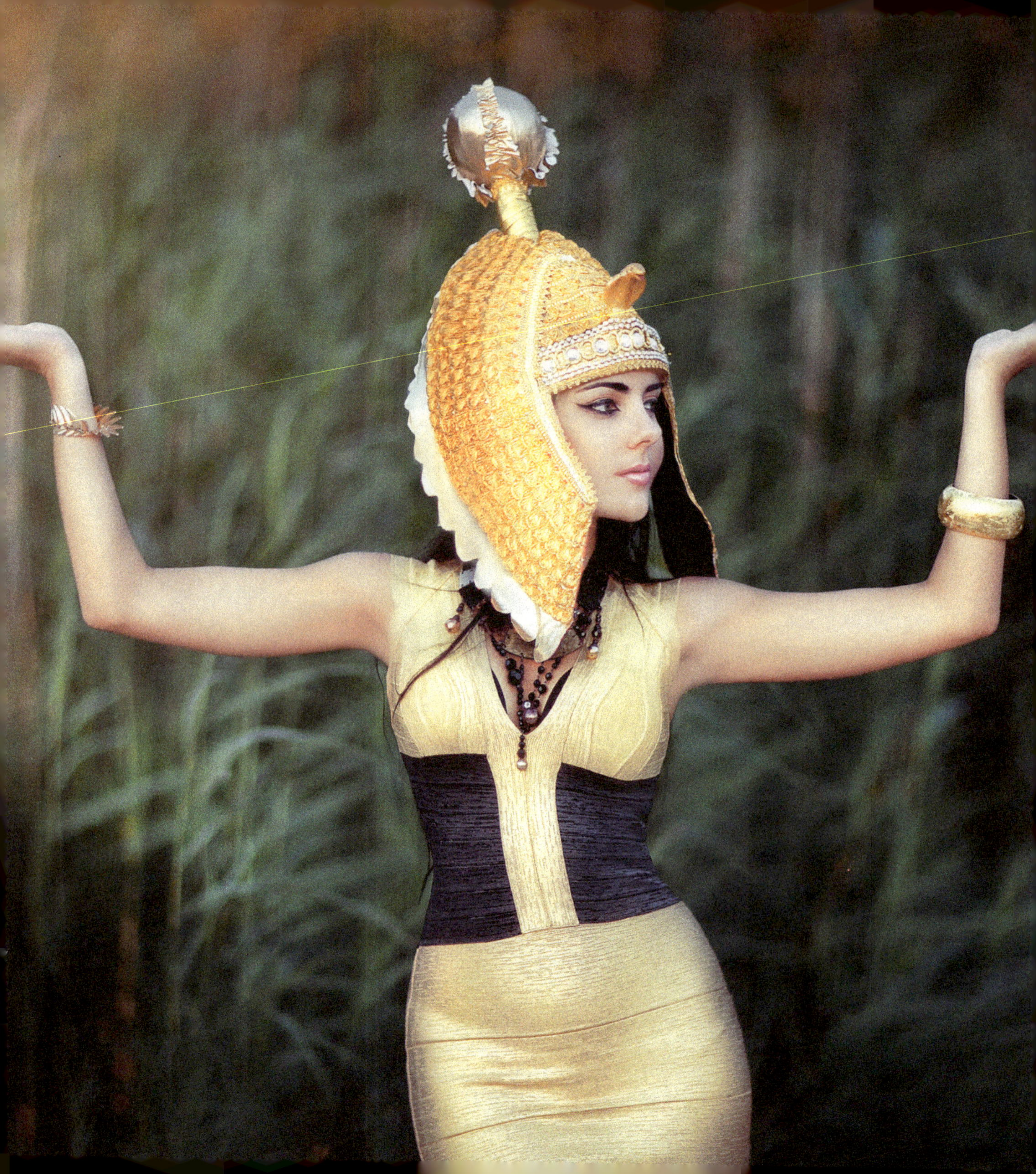

HOW LONG HAVE PEOPLE BEEN USING GOLD?

People have been decorating themselves with gold jewelry since 4,000 BC if not earlier. A woman from the Stone Age was found buried with a chain made of gold around her neck. Gold can be found in the jewelry and headdresses of ancient Egypt. Gold dental implants have been used since the time of the Celts. A Chinese king from 128 BC was placed in his tomb with chariots gilded with gold.

WHAT IS FOOL'S GOLD?

Pyrite, also called fool's gold, looks like gold but it isn't gold. Its powder is greenish-black while gold's powder still retains its gold color even when it's crushed or pulverized. Pyrite is still useful. During World War II it was used to make sulfuric acid, which has many uses as an industrial chemical. Today, it's still used to create batteries for cars, costume jewelry, and parts for machinery. Finding pyrite instead of gold can be somewhat disappointing, however it's a common occurrence that finding pyrite leads to nearby sources for both copper and real gold.

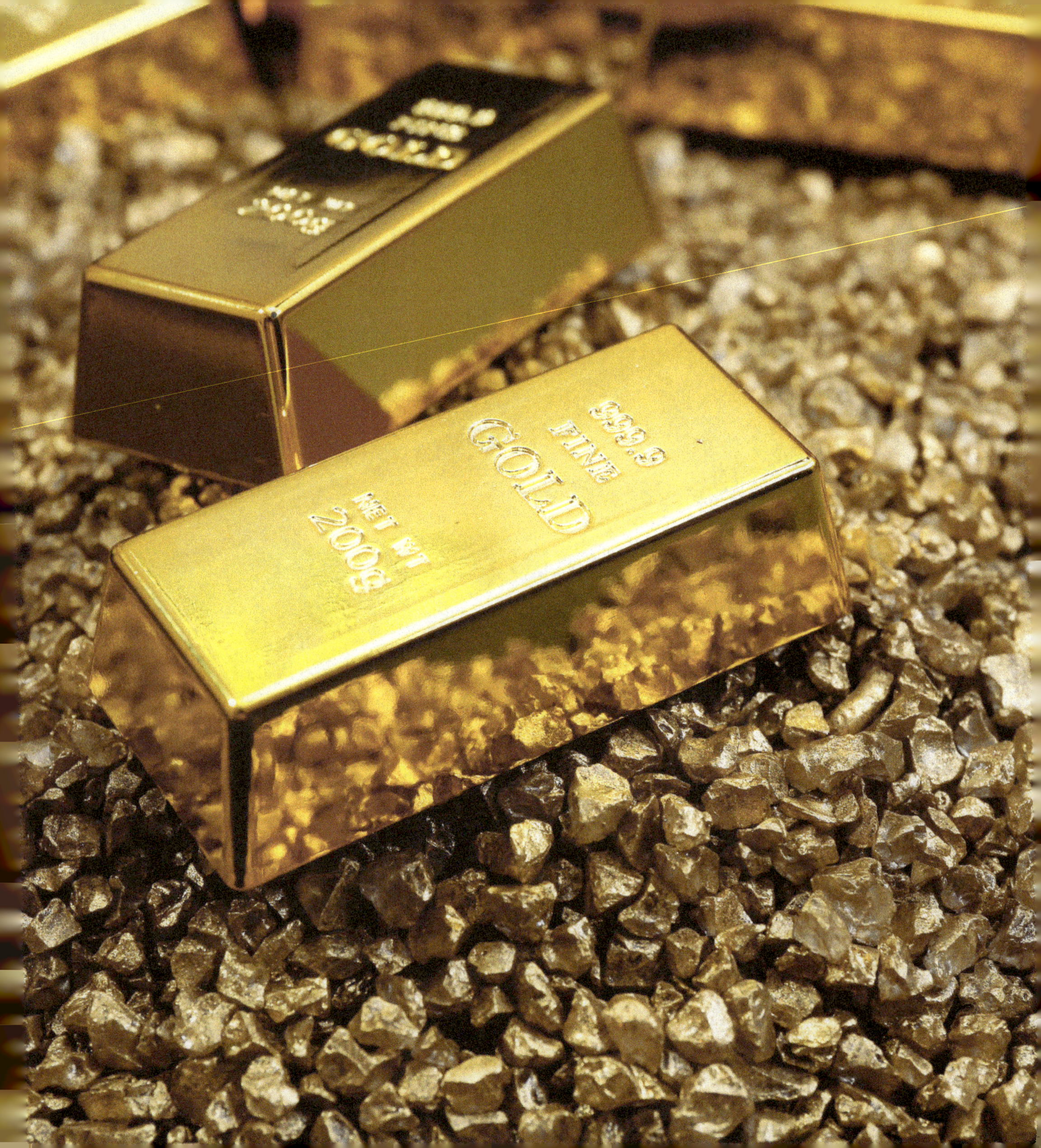
999.9
FINE
GOLD
NET WT
200g

WHERE DID GOLD COME FROM?

The intense heat of supernova explosions and the collision of neutron stars create metallic elements including gold. Astronomers think that gold-rich meteors bombarded the Earth about four billion years ago bringing billions of tons of gold to Earth.

WHAT IS A CARAT?

In the marketplaces of Ancient Asia, carob seeds were used to measure gold and this is where the word "carat" comes from. Because gold is so soft, it generally is mixed with other metals to create jewelry.

24 Carat Gold pieces

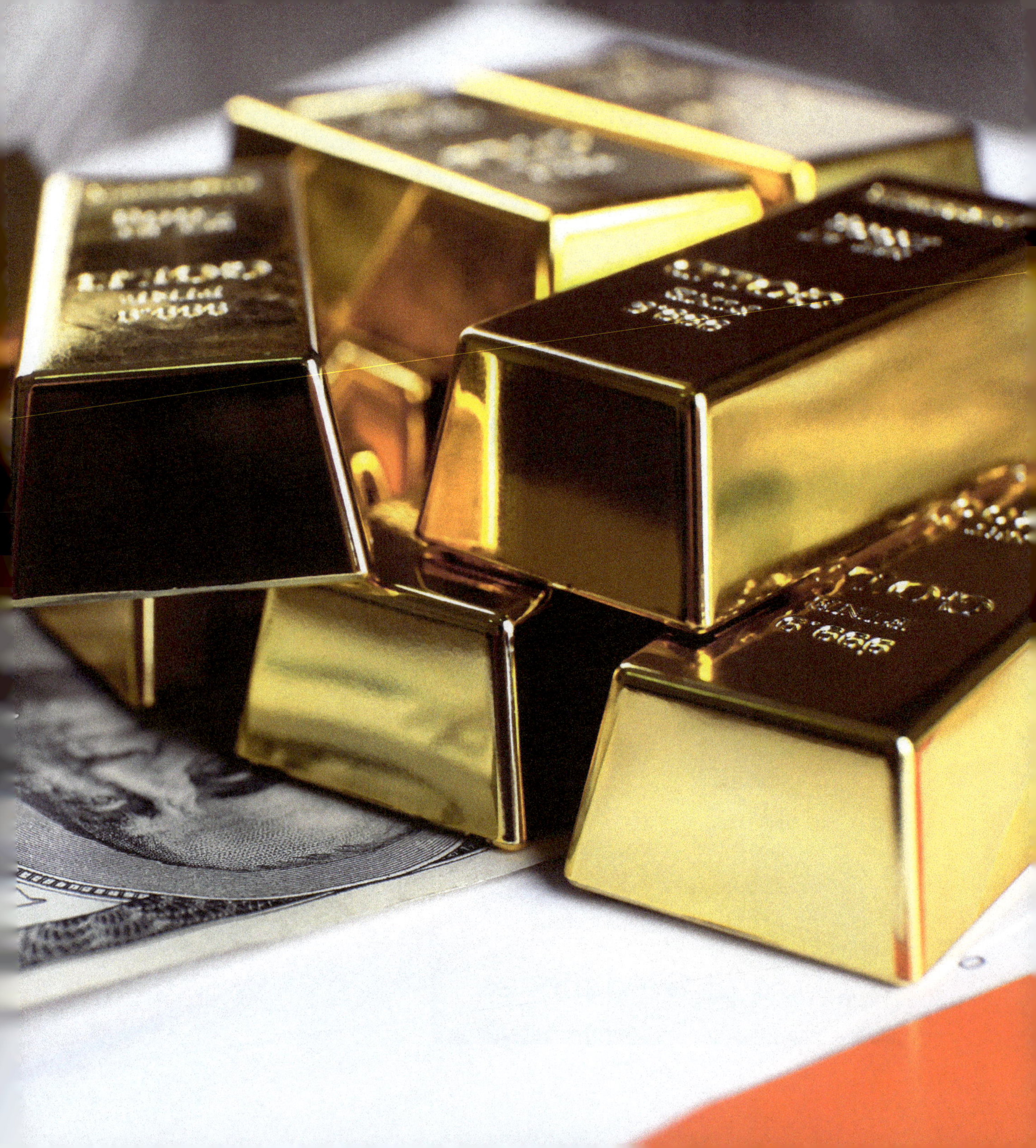

As other metals are mixed with gold, the number of carats drops. For example, the gold bars stored in Fort Knox are considered to be 24-carat gold, because they are almost pure gold. They are made of 99.95% pure gold and 0.05% alloy. If you buy a 12-karat necklace, it's only about 50% pure gold and the remaining mixture used to make it is other metals.

HOW MUCH GOLD IS IN FORT KNOX?

The United States Government opened up a depository for gold reserves in 1937 and named it after the very first Secretary of the Treasury. For some reason, in the 1970s a rumor was started that the gold the US had was no longer there. A special tour was arranged only for congressmen and select journalists to see just one room of the gold vault that houses over 36,000 gold bars. It's estimated that Fort Knox has $180 billion in gold bars.

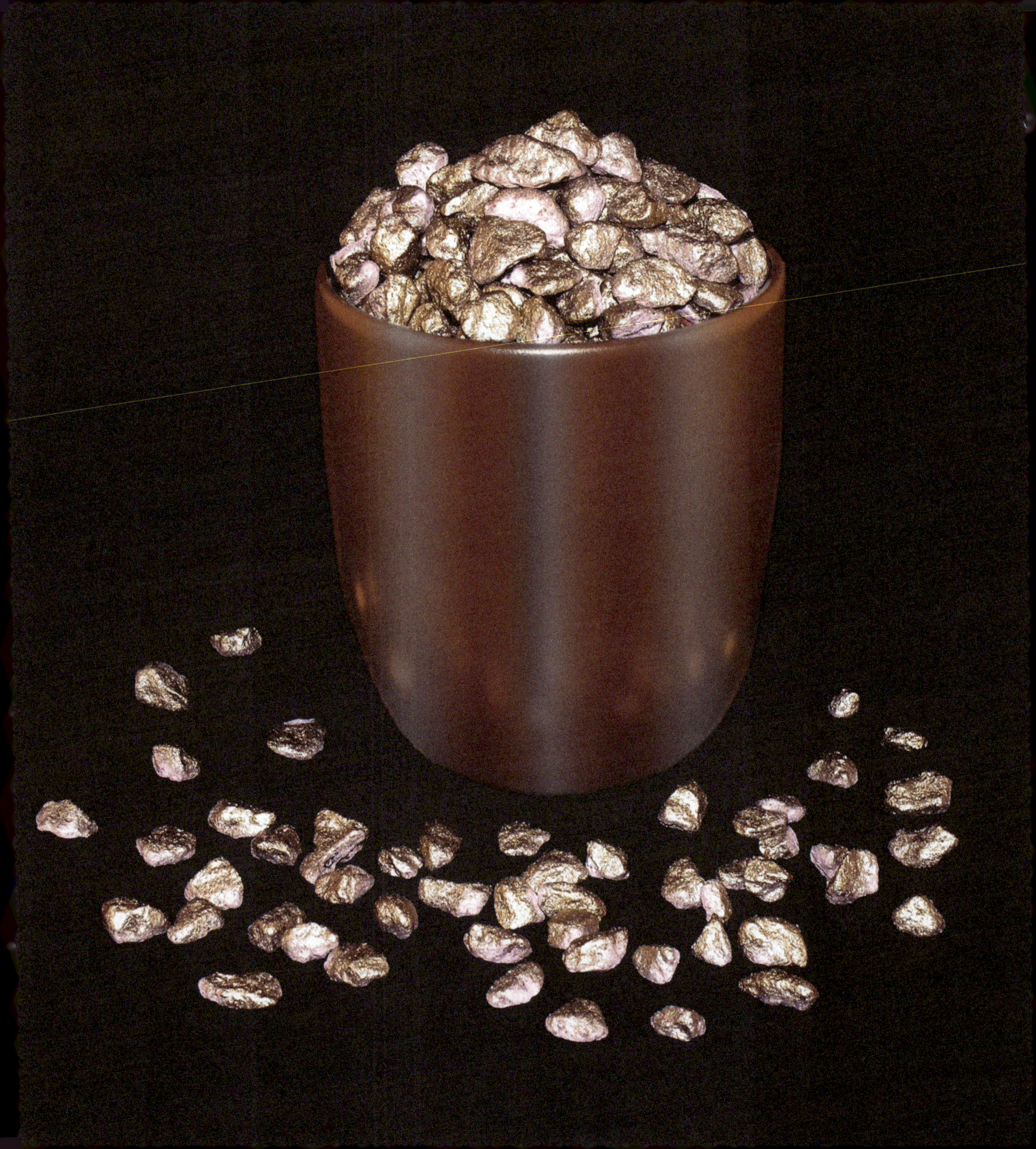

FASCINATING FACTS ABOUT GOLD

Just one ounce of gold can be hammered thinly enough to cover a surface that is 9 square meters or 96.9 square feet.

Just one ounce of gold can be made into an ultra-thin gold wire that is 50 miles or 80.5 kilometers long.

You can eat gold leaf and flakes. Gourmet shops add these to pastries for decorations. The gold doesn't hurt your stomach and isn't digested but just passes right through your body!

Gold Flakes

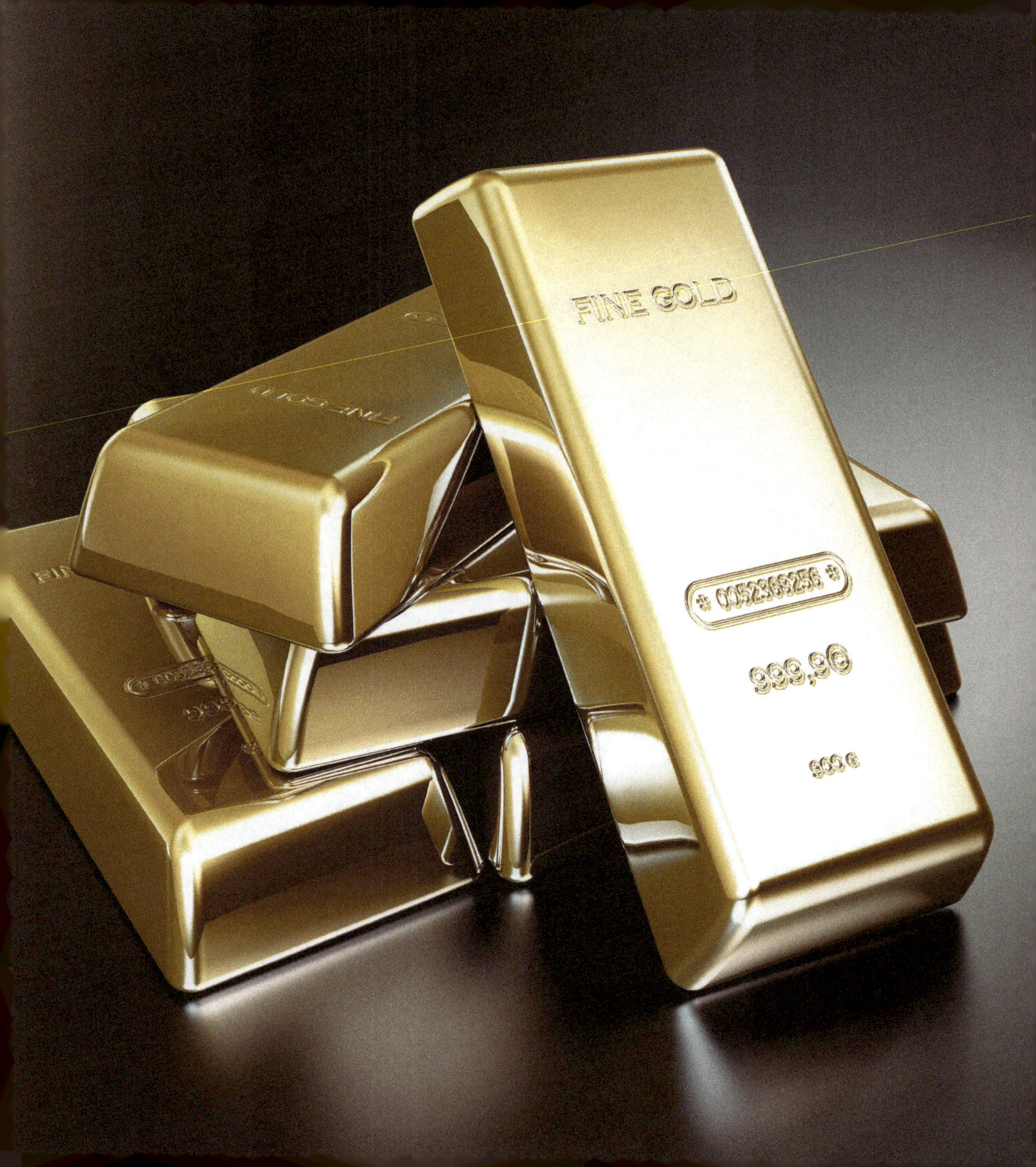
FINE GOLD

The largest gold crystal in the world is about the diameter of a standard golf ball. It weighs about 7.7 ounces and is valued at 1.5 million dollars.

One of the results of earthquakes is that they can help to filter out gold. The water left in faults eventually evaporates and sometimes gold is deposited there.

FINE
GOLD
999.9

121,4

120,9

1 ounce gold ingots

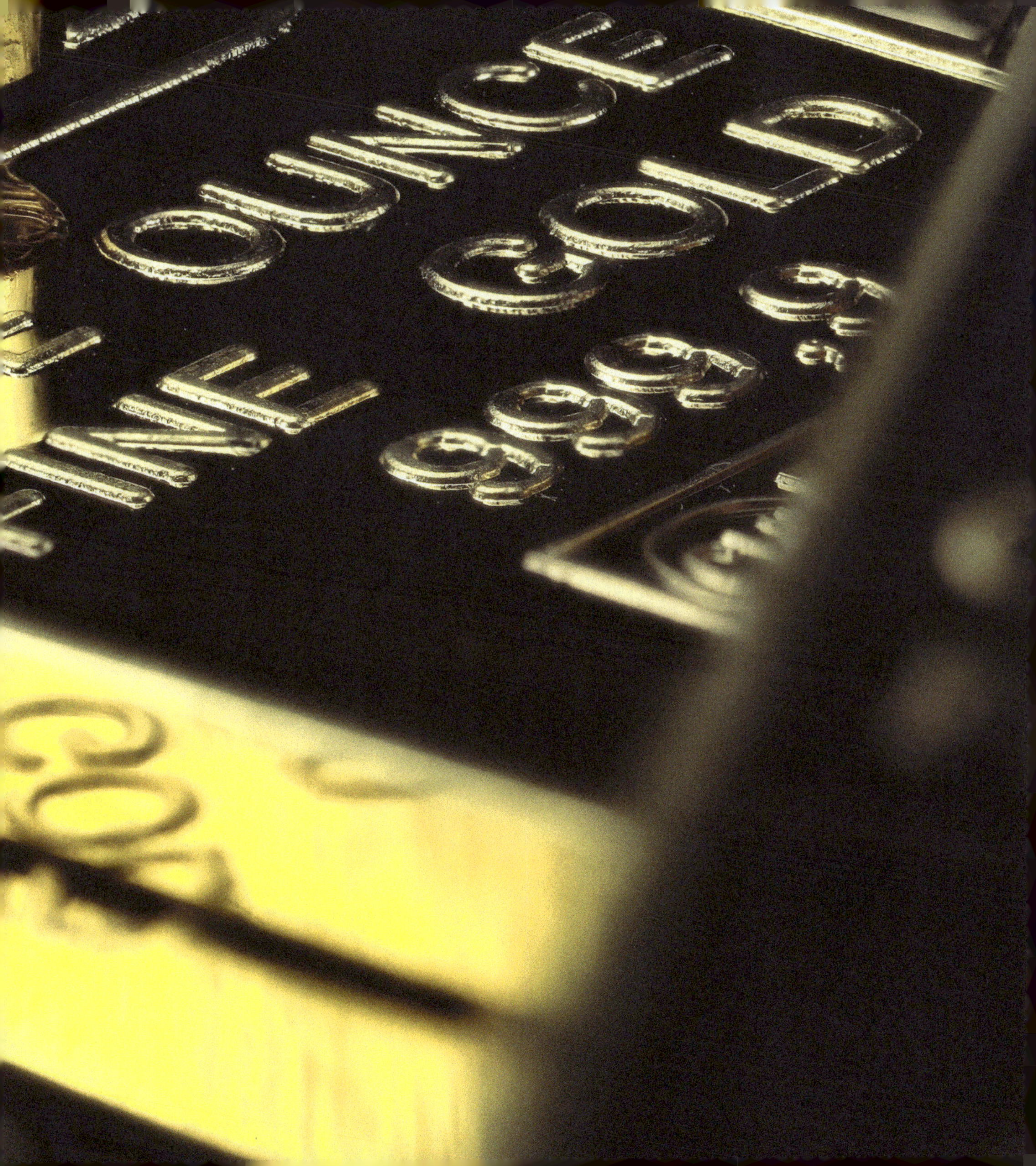
OUNCE
GOLD

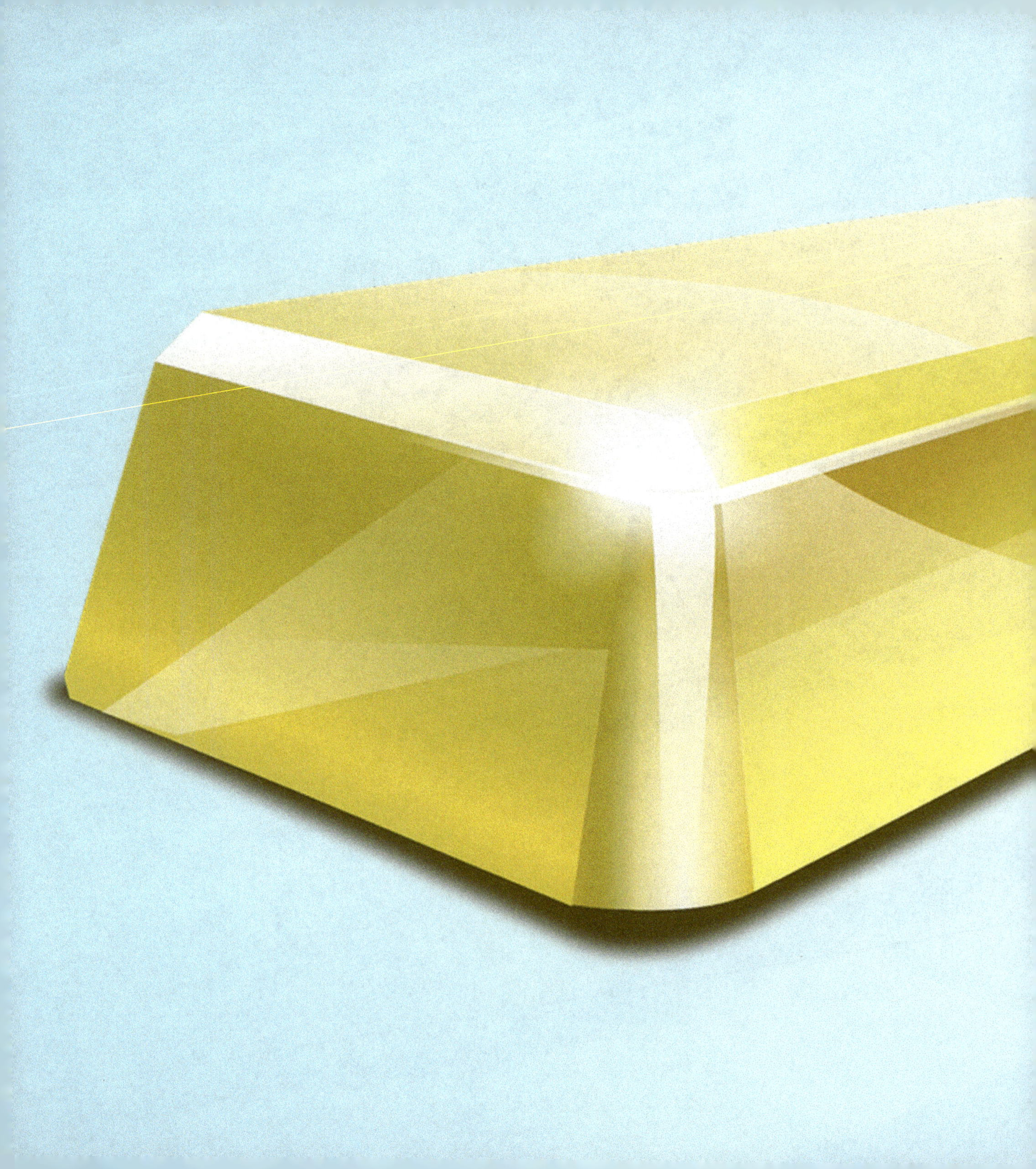

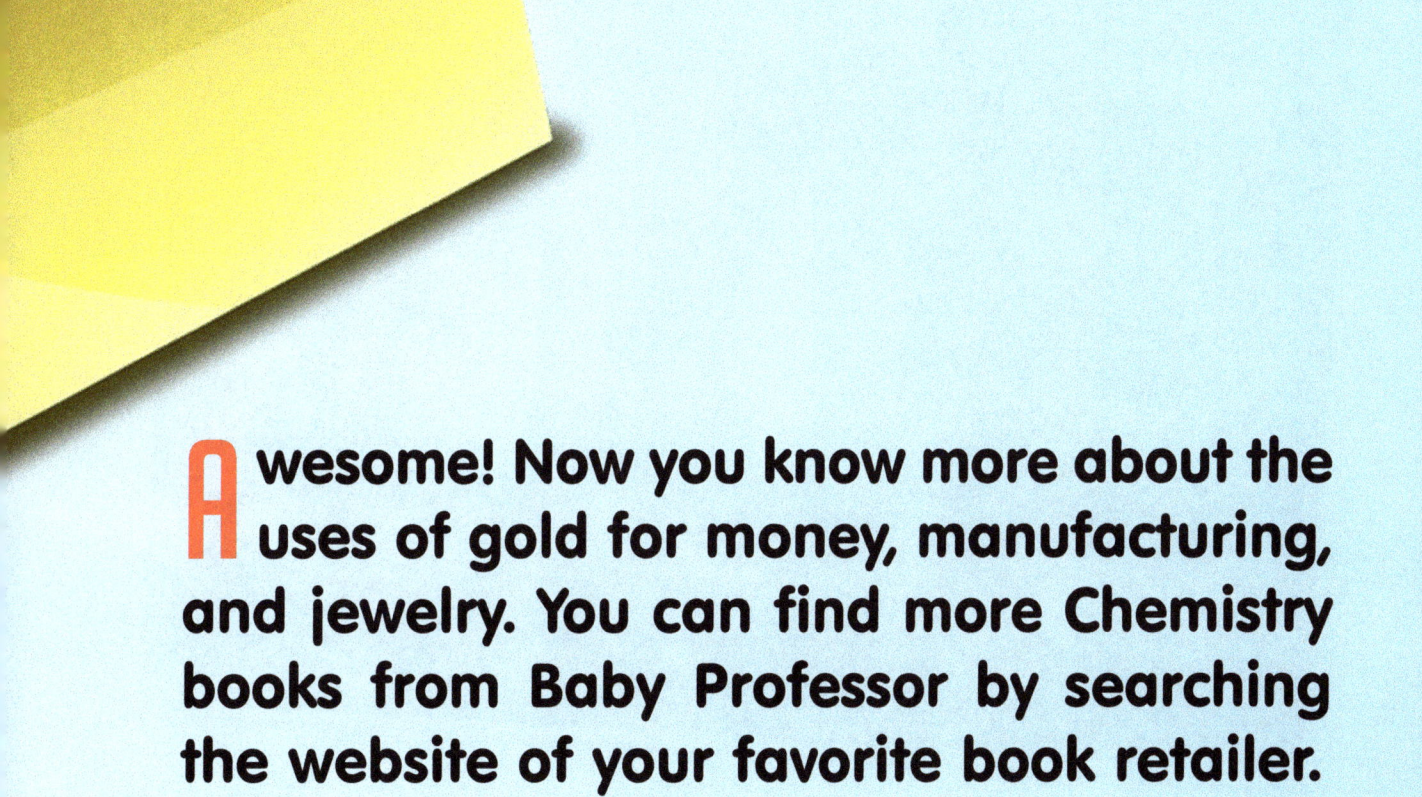

Awesome! Now you know more about the uses of gold for money, manufacturing, and jewelry. You can find more Chemistry books from Baby Professor by searching the website of your favorite book retailer.

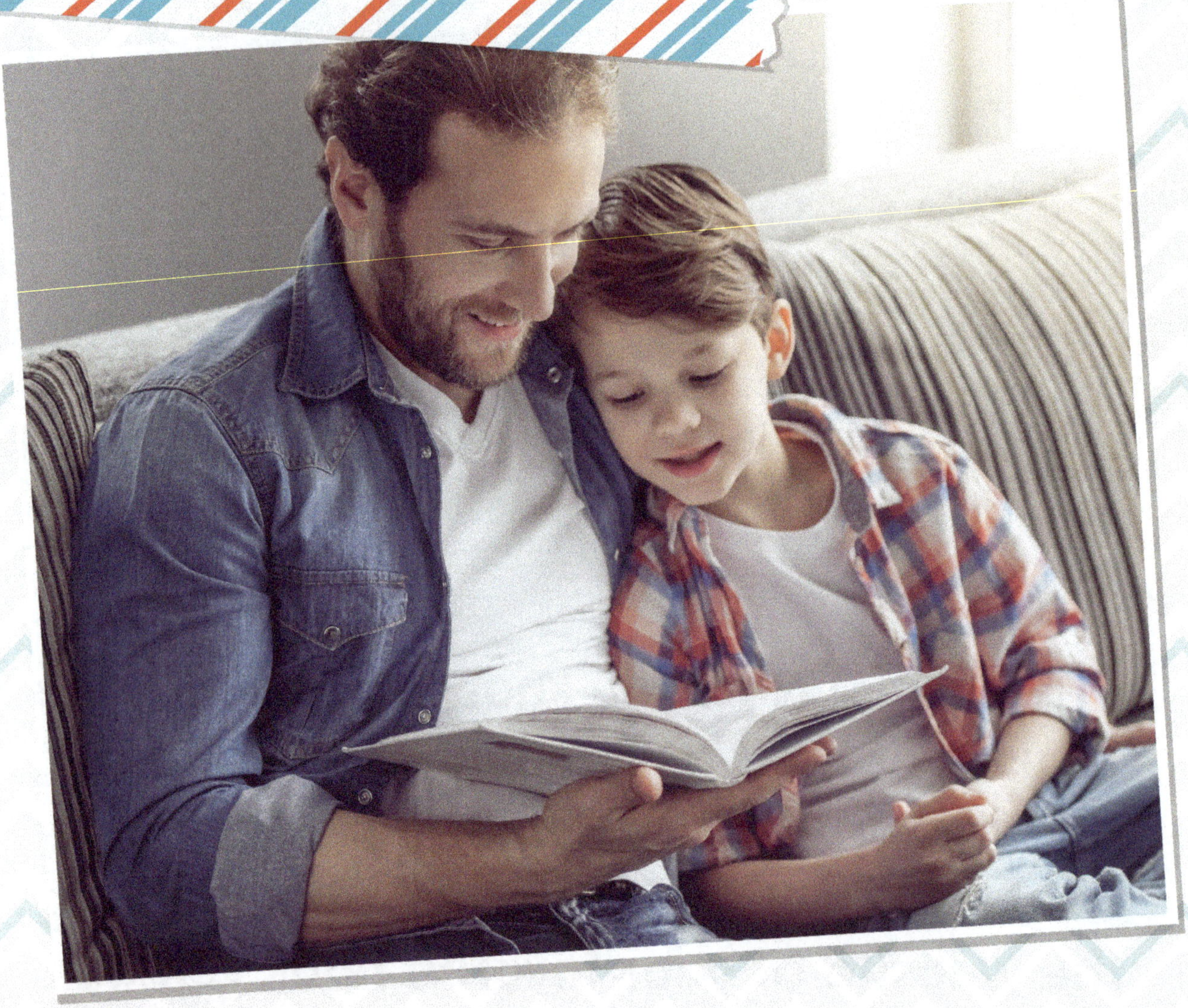

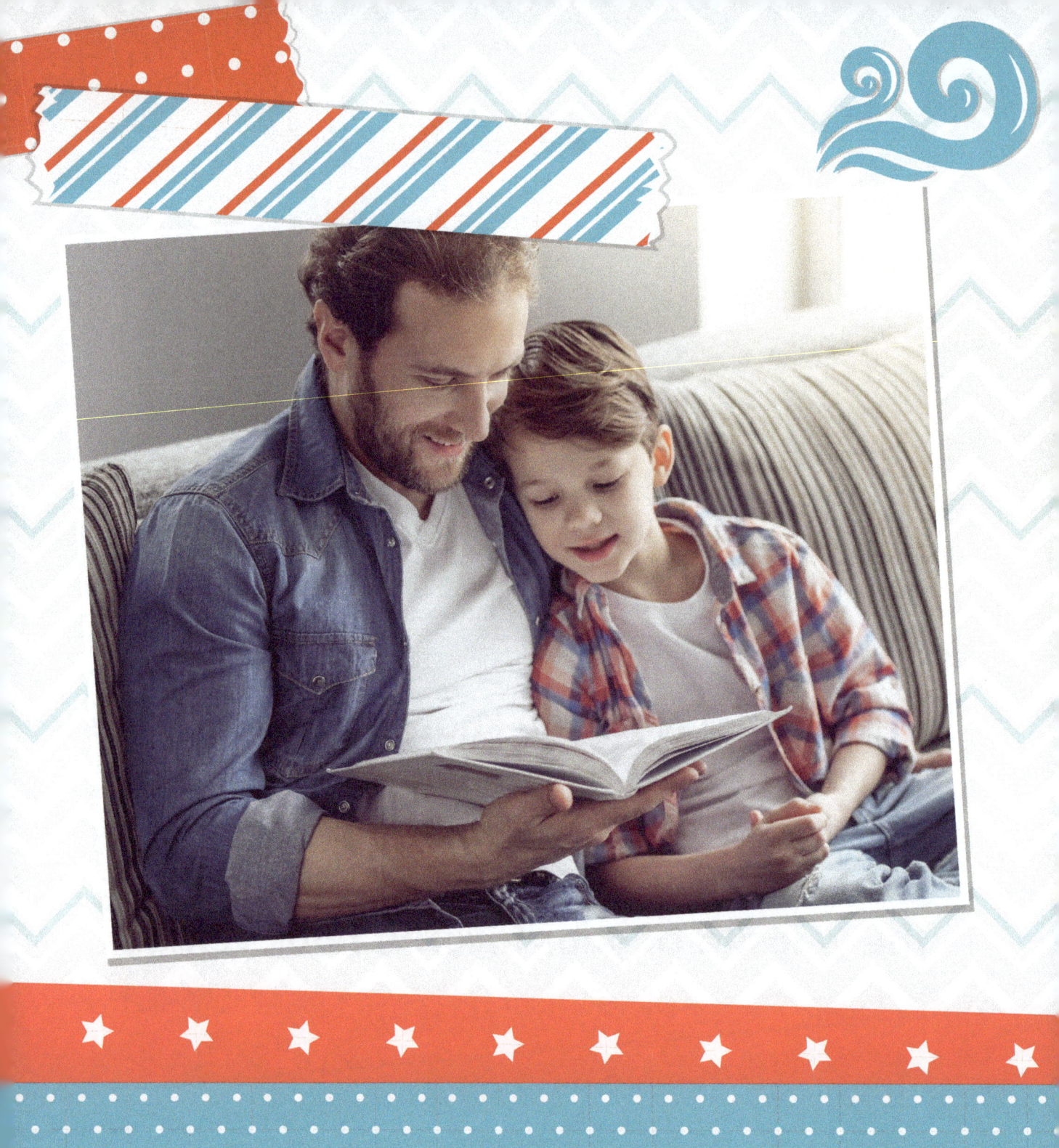

Visit

BABY PROFESSOR
EDUCATION KIDS

www.BabyProfessorBooks.com

to download Free Baby Professor eBooks and view
our catalog of new and exciting Children's Books

Lightning Source UK Ltd.
Milton Keynes UK
UKHW050918100822
407108UK00005B/53

9 781541 913707